RELIGIONS TO inSPiRE

for KS3

Buddhism

Diane Kolka

Series editor: Steve Clarke

DYNAMIC LEARNING

HODDER EDUCATION
AN HACHETTE UK COMPANY

For my children, Hannah, Laura, Ben and Rachel, husband, Richard, and Mum, Nancy, with love.

Orders: please contact Bookpoint Ltd, 130 Milton Park, Abingdon, Oxon OX14 4SB. Telephone: (44) 01235 827720. Fax: (44) 01235 400454. Lines are open 9.00–5.00, Monday to Saturday, with a 24-hour message answering service. Visit our website at www.hoddereducation.co.uk

© Diane Kolka 2012
First published in 2012 by
Hodder Education,
An Hachette UK Company
338 Euston Road
London NW1 3BH

Impression number   5 4 3 2
Year   2016 2015 2014 2013

Cover photo © andreas reimann – Fotolia.com
Illustrations by Barking Dog Art and Peter Lubach
Typeset in Minion regular 12.5pt/15pt by Wooden Ark
Printed in Dubai

A catalogue record for this title is available from the British Library

ISBN: 978 1444 12220 6

Contents

1.1 Who was the Buddha?

Learning objectives

You will ...
- learn some beliefs and facts about the Buddha
- compare and contrast ways in which the Buddha is shown in art
- investigate characteristics of the Buddha.

Siddattha Gotama was given the title 'The Buddha' – it means 'the **Enlightened** One'. **Enlightenment** is a deep understanding of how to be truly happy and free.

Siddattha Gotama was born in the part of India that is now called Nepal.

Siddattha Gotama was born as a prince. As a young man, he led a luxurious lifestyle; he thought he had everything a person could ever want.

Siddattha was protected from the natural sufferings of life, such as **poverty**, illness and death, by his father until his late twenties when he left the palace. His father did not want Siddattha to know that it was normal for people to suffer.

This picture shows the Buddha meditating. The position of his hand shows that he is teaching.

After enlightenment the Buddha preached the **Dhamma** (his teachings about life) to help others achieve enlightenment until he died. His death is called his **Parinibbana**.

While meditating under a fig tree (later known as the **Bodhi tree**) Siddattha became enlightened; he realised what the solutions to the problems of life were and came to the conclusion that the **Middle Way** was the way to happiness. From this point, Siddattha was known as the **Buddha**.

Siddattha realised that the extremes of a strict or a luxurious lifestyle did not lead to happiness; instead they led to suffering.

Siddattha made more visits outside the palace; during these he saw an old man, a sick man, a dead man and a wise man. These helped him to realise the truth about life. Buddhists refer to them as the **Four Sights**.

This picture shows Siddattha as a young prince coming across the Four Sights.

Knowledge check

1 What does the title 'Buddha' mean?

2 Where was Siddattha born?

3 What kind of life did Siddattha have as a young man?

4 What things did Siddattha see that made him realise the truth about life?

5 What did Siddattha say was the way to happiness?

6 What happened to Siddattha while he meditated under the Bodhi tree?

7 What was the Parinibbana of the Buddha?

Activity A

Write an article about the Buddha for a school newspaper. Include:

• a description of how he was brought up
• a description of what happened to him.

The Buddha in art

This picture shows the Buddha holding his hands in a position called Earth touching. This illustrates the time after he was enlightened and he is calling the Earth to witness what has happened to him.

This picture shows the reclining Buddha at his death (Parinibbana). The flame above his head represents enlightenment.

Activity B

1 Look at the pictures of the Buddha (on pages 4, 6 and 7). Each picture shows a characteristic of the Buddha. A characteristic is a distinguishing feature and is used to describe something or someone. Some ways a Buddhist might describe the Buddha include calm, loving, peaceful, human, **compassionate**, faithful, honest and caring. Can you think of any more?

2 Which characteristics or descriptions are shown in the pictures?

3 Which three characteristics do you think would have been the most important in the life of the Buddha? Try to give reasons for your choices.

This picture shows a statue of a Buddha sitting on a lotus flower, with his hands in a meditation position. It is called the Lotus Buddha (or Meditation Buddha).

This picture shows a statue of the Laughing Buddha with children.

Activity C

1 Choose two of the pictures from pages 4, 6 and 7 that interest you. Write down at least three reasons why you have chosen them.

2 In groups discuss the various pictures and decide which one your group thinks is the best one to show the characteristics of the Buddha and why.

3 Explain the decision your group made to the rest of the class in a brief presentation.

Activity D

1 Find some more pictures that show different characteristics and features of the Buddha. You could look in books or search the Internet. Type 'Buddha' in a search engine and click the 'images' option.

2 Investigate when these images were created, by whom and why.

3 Make a display using the pictures and include explanations of what each picture shows about the Buddha.

1.2 What is the Tipitaka?

Learning objectives

You will ...
- learn what the Tipitaka is
- understand what the Tipitaka contains
- explain why the Tipitaka is important for Buddhists.

The **Tipitaka** is a collection of scriptures used by Buddhists. The word Tipitaka can be translated to mean 'three baskets'. Some think that it is called the 'three baskets' because the scriptures were written on long leaves sewn together with boards either side of the leaves to keep them flat. These were then stored in baskets. Others think it is simply because the writings can be divided into three sections. The Tipitaka is also called the **Pali Canon** because it was originally written in Pali, which is an ancient language that was used in the Indian subcontinent when the Buddha lived.

The writings within the Tipitaka were passed on by **oral tradition** (stories told from one generation to the next) from after the Buddha died until some point between 3BCE and 1BCE when they were written down.

The Tipitaka is respected by all Buddhists because it contains the teachings of the Buddha. However, it is especially used by Theravadin Buddhists (a group originating from Sri Lanka and South East Asia).

A copy of the Tipitaka, written on palm leaves.

Knowledge check

1 What is the Tipitaka?
2 What does the word 'Tipitaka' mean?
3 Why do some people think the scriptures can be referred to as the 'three baskets'?
4 What else is the Tipitaka called and why?
5 What are the three types of writing in the Tipitaka called?
6 When was the Tipitaka written?
7 Who is the Tipitaka used by?
8 Why do Buddhists use the Tipitaka?

The Three Baskets

The three sections or baskets within the Tipitaka are the Vinaya Pitaka, the Sutta Pitaka and the Abhidhamma Pitaka.

- The Vinaya Pitaka: this section contains 227 rules for Buddhist monks (**bhikkhus**).
- The Sutta Pitaka: this section contains the Buddhist teachings. It also has stories about the Buddha.
- The Abhidhamma Pitaka: this section contains detailed explanations of what the Buddhist teachings mean.

A monk holding a wooden printing block from the Tipitaka housed in the Haein Temple in Hapcheon, South Korea.

The Parable of the Blind Man and the Elephant

The Parable of the Blind Man and the Elephant is a story found in the Tipitaka. The Buddha told the story because people were arguing about which preachers' teachings were correct.

Once upon a time there was a certain raja who called to his servant and said, 'Come, good fellow, go and gather together in one place all the men from this city who were born blind, and show them an elephant.'

'Very good, sire,' replied the servant, and he did as he was told. When the blind men were all gathered together he brought in an elephant.

'Here is an elephant,' he said and he led one man to one of the elephant's ears, another to the trunk, another to one of the elephant's feet, one to the elephant's side, one to its tail. The servant told each blind man that this was the elephant.

When the blind men had felt the elephant, the raja went to each of them and asked, 'Well, blind man, tell me, what sort of thing is an elephant?'

The man who had been led to the elephant's side said: 'The elephant is just like a wall.' The one who had felt the ear said: 'It's not at all like a wall, it's much too thin. Feel how it flaps! It's like a sail.' The one who felt the trunk said: 'The elephant is like a thick piece of rope.' The one who felt its feet said: 'No, it's not like a rope, or a sail or a wall – it is clearly a type of pillar; strong and sturdy.' The one who felt the tail said: 'I am certain that the elephant is just like a flywhisk.'

Then they began to quarrel, shouting, 'Yes it is!', 'No, it is not!', 'An elephant is not that!', 'Yes, it is like that!' and so on, until they started to fight each other.

Activity A

Read the Parable of the Blind Man and the Elephant.

1 What do you think it is meant to teach?

2 Do you think the parable is a good way of teaching people?

3 Do you think this parable is important for people living today? Why?

4 Re-tell the parable using something that people would be familiar with today, rather than an elephant.

Activity B

1 Which of the sections of the Tipitaka is most important for Buddhists? Give reasons why.

2 Why do the monks and nuns require the Vinaya Pitaka?

3 Find out why the writings within the Abhidhamma Pitaka are kept separately from the other two sections.

4 Why do you think Buddhists needed to write these scriptures rather than keep retelling them?

5 Explain why telling stories is a good way of teaching.

Sayings of the Buddha

Three things cannot be long hidden: the Sun, the Moon, and the truth.

The truthful one avoids and abstains from tale-bearing.

A wise person is characterised by his actions, and a fool by his.

He who envies others does not obtain peace of mind.

When words are both true and kind, they can change our world.

To understand everything is to forgive everything.

Activity C

1. In pairs, read and discuss the sayings of the Buddha above.

2. Think about what each saying means and whether you think it is a useful teaching.

3. On your own, copy this table into your notes and complete it for three of the sayings.

Saying of the Buddha	What does this mean?	Reasons why it is useful or not useful
1		
2		
3		

4. In pairs, compare your tables and add anything that you had not already written.

A dog is not considered a good dog because he is a good barker. A man is not considered a good man because he is a good talker.

This quotation of the Buddha is typical as it is short and brief yet still has a deep meaning that can be contemplated upon and put into practice.

Activity D

1. Explain why it is a good idea to try to live according to the sayings of the Buddha.

2. Explain why it might be difficult to try to live according to the sayings of the Buddha.

3. You could find out more of the Buddha's sayings to help you with your response. They are called the Dhammapada. You could try finding them on the Internet.

1.3 How do Buddhists worship?

Learning objectives

You will ...
- learn what worship is
- understand the ways that Buddhists worship
- understand why worship is important for Buddhists.

Buddhists do not believe in an all-powerful God. Nor do they **worship** the Buddha who was, after all, only a man. When they worship, they concentrate on trying to develop some of the characteristics of the Buddha – wisdom, kindness and courage. They also try to understand the Dhamma at a very deep level.

Worship is done in many different ways: some ways are different because of differences in Buddhist groups and some ways are different because of personal preferences. Buddhists sometimes call worship **puja**.

- Some Buddhists say prayers in private.
- Some Buddhists join with other Buddhists in a **vihara** (monastery) to worship.
- Some Buddhists perform worship when meditating.
- Some Buddhists worship by celebrating Buddhist festivals.
- Some Buddhists use prayer beads (**mala**).
- Some Buddhists read passages from the scriptures.
- Some Buddhists chant **mantras**.
- Some Buddhists produce **mandalas**.

Shrines vary in size and content. However, they always provide a focal point for puja.

Shrines can be found in many Buddhist homes and viharas. Shrines usually include:

- An image of the Buddha: to provide inspiration and represent enlightenment.
- Offering bowls: to show respect to the Buddha and his teachings. They may contain food and drink, or just water.
- Flowers: to show that nothing in life stays the same. (Flowers bloom and die.)
- Incense: spreading scent, just as the effects of good deeds spread.
- Candles: a symbol of enlightenment.
- Bells: to mark different stages in the worship.

Different representations of the Buddha.

Different representations of the Buddha.

Knowledge check

1 What is Buddhist worship?

2 What name is given to Buddhist worship?

3 Why do Buddhists worship?

4 Why are there lots of different ways of worshipping?

5 What is the name given to the beads used in Buddhist prayer?

6 Where might Buddhists go to worship?

The different hand positions (**muddas**) on a Buddha image can show different things: meditation, teaching, generosity, wisdom, fearlessness and reassurance.

Activity A

1 Draw a diagram of a shrine and then label it to show the various items in it.

2 Draw a table to show the different things found in a shrine and what they symbolise to Buddhists.

Activity B

1 Look at the different Buddha images on pages 13–14. What do all the images have in common?

2 Write some reasons why you think some of the same elements are found on most Buddha images.

3 What are the differences between the images?

4 Write some reasons why some of the elements on Buddha images are different.

Activity C

1 In pairs, discuss the kind of hand shapes that you could make to indicate the characteristic of meditation, teaching or generosity.

2 Draw a diagram of the hand shape you have decided on. Explain why you think it shows the characteristic chosen.

3 How do you think the images of the Buddha and the various muddas help Buddhists worship?

Activity D

Some people think that Buddhists do not need to worship at all.

1 What arguments would you give against this point of view?

2 What arguments would you give to agree with this point of view?

3 Do you think it is possible for all Buddhists to worship in the same way?

1.4 What is the Sangha?

Learning objectives

You will ...
- learn what the Sangha is
- understand what the Sangha does
- understand the importance of the Sangha for Buddhists.

The word **Sangha** means group or community. In Buddhism, it can refer to two things:

1. Everyone who follows the teachings of the Buddha (the Dhamma).

2. Buddhist monks (bhikkhus) and nuns (**bhikkhunis**), who give up family life in order to devote their lives completely to following the Dhamma.

What does the Sangha do?

The Sangha began as a small group of followers who travelled round with the Buddha. As time went on the followers formed groups and lived together. They introduced rules to help them live an orderly Buddhist life.

The Sangha provides a community where other Buddhists can learn from one another and practise Buddhist teachings away from the rest of society. This is also called 'taking refuge'.

Lay Buddhists (Buddhists who are not monks or nuns) take food and other gifts to the Sangha. They gain **merit** from being generous and are following the teachings of the Buddha to be selfless.

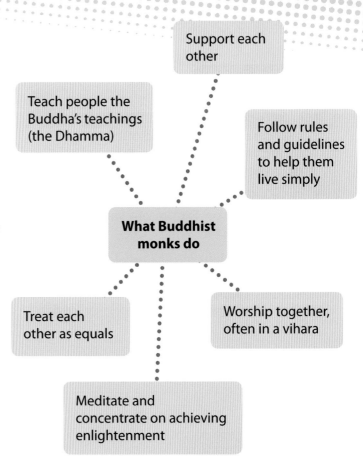

Support each other

Teach people the Buddha's teachings (the Dhamma)

Follow rules and guidelines to help them live simply

What Buddhist monks do

Treat each other as equals

Worship together, often in a vihara

Meditate and concentrate on achieving enlightenment

Knowledge check

1. What does the word 'Sangha' mean?

2. What are the two different uses of the word Sangha?

3. Which words are sometimes used for monks and nuns?

4. What does the Sangha do?

Activity A

1. Copy and complete the table below into your exercise books.

What the Sangha does	Why this is important for Buddhists

What is it like to be a monk or a nun?

Being a monk has allowed me to spend all my time following the path to enlightenment.

I try to spread the teachings of the Buddha.

I spend time every day growing food for the rest of the Sangha and at the end of the day I study the Buddhist scriptures.

I spend my time with other monks and nuns discussing the best way to live a Buddhist life in modern western society.

I am able to teach other people how to meditate so that they can become much calmer people.

I like being able to spend time in meditation and reflection every day.

All Buddhists keep **Five Precepts** (guidelines for living). These are:
- not killing
- not stealing
- not hurting others through sex
- not lying
- not becoming **intoxicated**.

Bhikkhus and bhikkhunis keep five extra precepts:
- not to eat in the afternoon
- not to take part in entertainments (dancing/singing)
- not to wear jewellery or perfume
- not to have a luxurious bed
- not to handle money.

Activity B

1 Imagine you are a journalist reporting for a children's TV programme. You have to present a report on what the monks and the nuns in the Sangha do.

2 You might need to do some research and write down notes to help you. Think about how to present your report in an entertaining but informative manner. Present it to the class.

Activity C

1 Read the descriptions in the photo from the monks and nuns describing their lives. Think of any questions you would ask them about what they do.

2 Compare your questions in small groups and try to answer some of them.

Activity D

1 Produce a poster or PowerPoint that could be used to explain what the Sangha is.

2 Include descriptions of the different things that monks and nuns do.

3 Try to include some reasons why the Sangha is important for all Buddhists (those in the Sangha and those who are lay Buddhists).

17

1.5 What is a vihara?

Learning objectives

You will ...
- learn what a vihara is
- understand what happens in a vihara
- understand the importance of a vihara for Buddhists.

A vihara is a gathering place for Buddhists. It is also the Buddhist place of worship, a place of education in Buddhism and a place where Buddhist monks and nuns may live.

Inside a vihara there will be a shrine room. This is the place where Buddhists will gather to perform puja. A vihara may have other areas such as:
- a library containing Buddhist scriptures, which are used for studying and teaching about Buddhism
- a meditation room
- a kitchen
- a garden and facilities for monks and nuns.

From the outside, the vihara may look like any other building, depending on what it was originally built for. If it has been built specially then traditionally the door will be south facing. It may have a **stupa** containing **relics**, and it may have a Bodhi tree.

The London Buddhist Vihara looks like any other building from the outside.

Knowledge check

1 What is a vihara?
2 What happens inside a vihara?
3 What room will all viharas have?
4 What other rooms might a vihara contain?
5 What might a vihara look like from the outside?

The Birmingham Buddhist Vihara has been purpose built and has many traditional features of a vihara.

Activity A

1 Why is it important that a vihara has a shrine room? Give reasons for your answer.

2 Copy and complete the table below.

Part of the vihara	What it is used for	Why it is important for Buddhists
Shrine room		
Library		
Meditation room		
Meeting hall		
Shoe rack		

Daily programme of a vihara

7.30am–8.00am	Puja and chanting
10am–11am	Buddhism for Beginners class – Library
11am–12.30	Sitting meditation in Meditation hall
11am– 5pm	Library open for personal study
12.30–1pm	Puja and chanting
2pm–3pm	Walking meditation in the garden
6pm–7pm	Buddhism for Advanced students – Library
7pm–9pm	Buddhist service, including readings, sermon, chanting and meditation – Shrine room

Activity B

1 Look at the various parts of a vihara described on page 18. Make a list of how the different parts are used.

2 Imagine you are a journalist and have been sent to write an article about what a vihara is and what happens in a vihara. Write down some questions that you would like to ask.

3 Think about how a Buddhist might answer your questions. Then write a magazine article about the vihara. Include details from the daily programme in a vihara and how the building helps Buddhists.

4 Or visit a vihara. Interview the people who use the vihara to get information to add to your article.

Activity D

1 In groups, make a list of all the roles/jobs that need to be completed in a vihara. Decide which are essential and which are not essential.

2 Design a set of posters to go on a vihara noticeboard to show the different things that happen in a vihara and why.

3 Write a leaflet to go with the posters that explains why the activities are essential to the Buddhists attending the vihara.

Activity C

1 In pairs write a list of the things that happen in a vihara.

2 Write an advert for a vihara. Include why someone might want to visit a vihara and what the rewards of going to a vihara might be.

1.6 What festivals do Buddhists celebrate?

Learning objectives

You will ...
- learn what festivals Buddhists celebrate
- understand what the different festivals celebrate
- analyse why the festivals are important.

Festivals are special celebrations. Buddhists celebrate to remember parts of the Buddhist faith. The Buddha said that Buddhists should 'meet together regularly and in large numbers' and this is what festivals encourage Buddhists to do.

Some festivals are celebrated by all Buddhists, for example Buddhist New Year and **Wesak**, which is also called Buddha Day. The different Buddhist groups also celebrate different festivals.

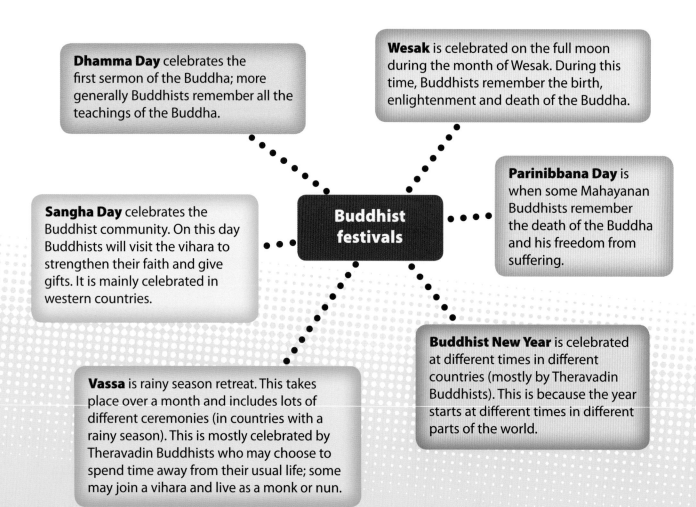

Dhamma Day celebrates the first sermon of the Buddha; more generally Buddhists remember all the teachings of the Buddha.

Wesak is celebrated on the full moon during the month of Wesak. During this time, Buddhists remember the birth, enlightenment and death of the Buddha.

Sangha Day celebrates the Buddhist community. On this day Buddhists will visit the vihara to strengthen their faith and give gifts. It is mainly celebrated in western countries.

Buddhist festivals

Parinibbana Day is when some Mahayanan Buddhists remember the death of the Buddha and his freedom from suffering.

Vassa is rainy season retreat. This takes place over a month and includes lots of different ceremonies (in countries with a rainy season). This is mostly celebrated by Theravadin Buddhists who may choose to spend time away from their usual life; some may join a vihara and live as a monk or nun.

Buddhist New Year is celebrated at different times in different countries (mostly by Theravadin Buddhists). This is because the year starts at different times in different parts of the world.

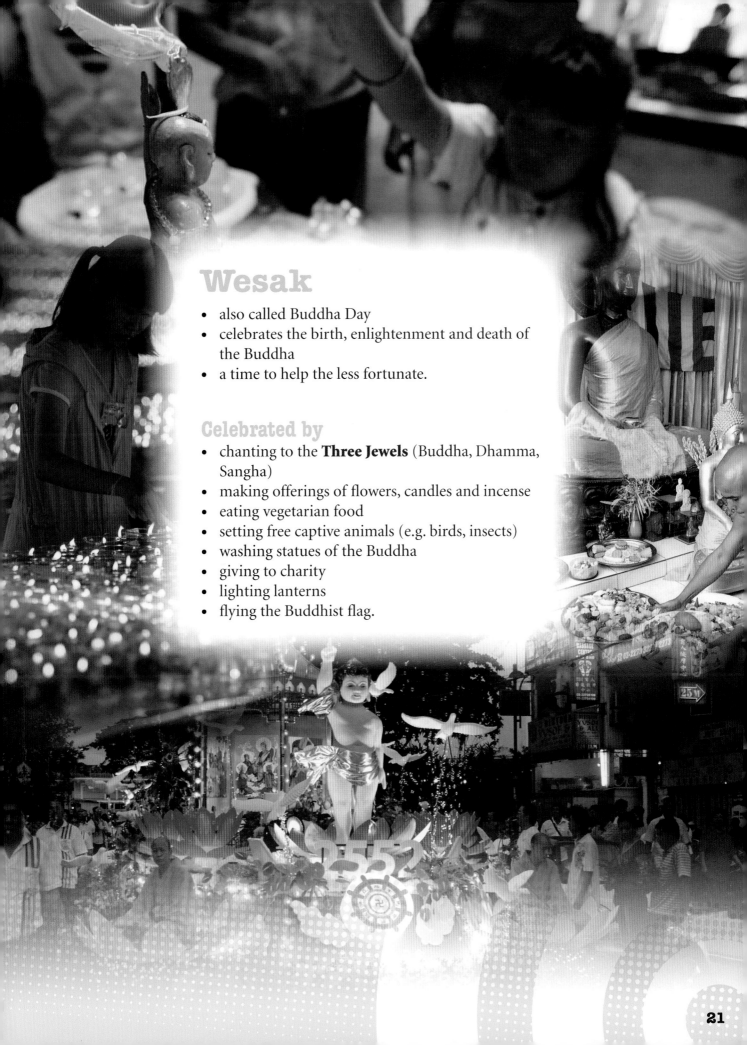

Wesak

- also called Buddha Day
- celebrates the birth, enlightenment and death of the Buddha
- a time to help the less fortunate.

Celebrated by

- chanting to the **Three Jewels** (Buddha, Dhamma, Sangha)
- making offerings of flowers, candles and incense
- eating vegetarian food
- setting free captive animals (e.g. birds, insects)
- washing statues of the Buddha
- giving to charity
- lighting lanterns
- flying the Buddhist flag.

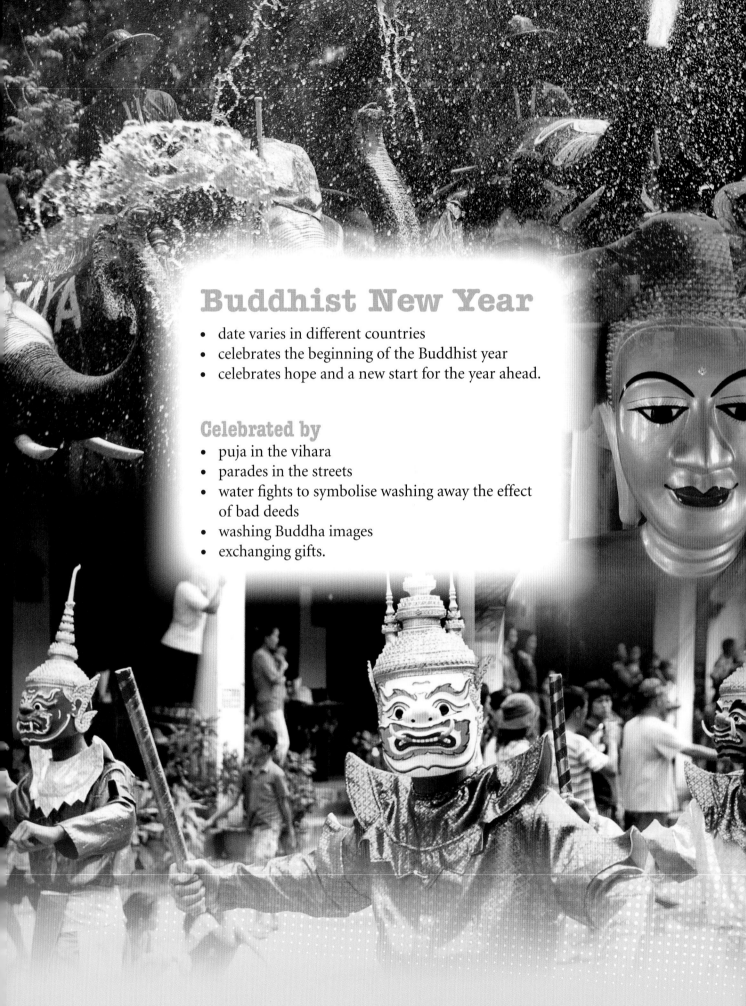

Buddhist New Year

- date varies in different countries
- celebrates the beginning of the Buddhist year
- celebrates hope and a new start for the year ahead.

Celebrated by

- puja in the vihara
- parades in the streets
- water fights to symbolise washing away the effect of bad deeds
- washing Buddha images
- exchanging gifts.

Knowledge check

1 What is a festival?

2 Why do Buddhists celebrate festivals?

3 Do all Buddhists celebrate the same festivals as each other? Give reasons why.

4 What does Wesak celebrate?

5 What does Dhamma Day celebrate?

6 Name one festival that only some Buddhists celebrate and explain why it is celebrated.

Activity A

1 Make a list of all the things that you celebrate in a year. They do not have to be religious but can include religious celebrations. You could do this as a diagram similar to the one on page 20.

2 Which of your celebrations is the one you enjoy the most? Describe in five lines what you do to celebrate it. Then write down three reasons why you enjoy celebrating it.

Activity B

1 Study the pictures of Wesak on page 21. What do the pictures tell you about how Buddhists feel about Wesak?

2 Do you have the same feelings about a festival that is important to you? Explain your reasons why or why not in three sentences.

Activity C

1 Look at the fact lists on Wesak (page 21) and New Year.

2 Draw a spidergram for each festival – include all the facts in the list and any more you can think of. If you can do this on a computer, include pictures to illustrate the various ways the festivals are celebrated.

3 Using your spidergram as notes, produce a booklet that could be used for teaching young children about either Wesak or New Year. This can be done on paper or on a computer.

Activity D

1 In small groups, discuss why you think Buddhists like celebrating festivals. Write down on a sheet of paper all the reasons your group can think of.

2 Do some research into the ways that Wesak and New Year have been celebrated in the past and are celebrated in various cultures.

3 Produce a poster to explain why you think Buddhists celebrate festivals like Wesak and New Year. Explain your poster to the others in the class when you have finished.

The big assignment

Objectives

- To research the history, purposes, architecture and features of a vihara and how it is used in worship.
- To use evidence from leaders in the vihara and/or worshippers to inform your findings.

Outcome

To produce an information pack that could be used in a vihara to give information to visitors about what it is and what it does.

You should include information about:

- the history of the vihara
- services and celebrations that take place in the vihara
- other uses for the building
- features of the vihara and how they are used
- symbols inside the vihara
- some of the feelings people have when they are in a vihara
- what the worshippers do to help other people in the community and the world.

Guidance

1 Work in groups of six or seven people. Each person should be given a specific job to do, and the rest of the group should support them in doing it.

2 Suggested jobs:

   a Asking the leaders of a local vihara (if you have one) to help you with the big assignment.

   b Writing questions to ask the leader of the vihara.

   c Asking the questions and writing up the answers.

   d Filming the interview.

   e Filming the vihara (if you are allowed to).

   f Photographing the various features of the vihara (if you are allowed to).

   g As an alternative, there are virtual tours of a vihara: visit www. reonline.org.uk and search in teacher resources for 'vihara'.

   h Writing up descriptions of the vihara and the objects inside it.

   i Drawing diagrams and plans to illustrate your descriptions and explanations.

   j Writing up explanations of why the objects are included in the vihara and explaining how they are used.

3 As a group, go through the evidence, i.e. the outcomes of each job, and for each one decide what needs to be done to finish it.

4 Remember to include instructions for visitors about how they should behave in a vihara (and why), and how they should treat the objects within a vihara (and why).

5 Your completed information pack should contain your findings in a variety of media: film, photographs, plans, diagrams and text.

6 Present your information pack to the leader of the vihara, and ask for feedback.

7 As a group, evaluate your pack: decide what you did well and what you could have improved.

Assessment

You will be assessed on:

✓ how well you use specialist vocabulary

✓ your ability to explain the importance of religious objects for worshippers

✓ your ability to explain how people should behave in a vihara, and why

✓ how you allocated roles, and how well you worked with others

✓ your evaluation of the success of your team.

2.1 What do Buddhists believe about life?

Learning objectives

You will ...
- learn about Buddhist beliefs about life
- make links between Buddhist beliefs about life and the sources of these beliefs
- assess the impact of beliefs about life on Buddhists.

All physical things change and do not last. Work hard to gain your freedom.

The nature of life

The **Buddha** taught that all things change – they are not permanent. They are always changing and nothing stays the same. Even human beings change: they are born, grow, get old and die. Buddhists do not believe that humans have a part of them that could be called a **soul**. Most believe that humans are made up of five categories or **khandhas**. These are: form, feelings, perception, mental developments and awareness. These categories join at birth to make a human being.

Samsara

Buddhists believe that life is a continuous round of birth, old age, death and rebirth. The word **samsara** means 'perpetual wandering'.

Samsara – the cycle of birth and death.

Kamma

Buddhists believe that a person is affected by their actions and the intention behind their actions. This is called **kamma**. The word kamma means action. Positive actions have positive influences on a person's life, and negative actions have negative influences.

For example, cheating in a test is bad kamma and will lead to unhappiness, whereas helping someone in need is good kamma and will lead to good fortune in the future.

Buddhists believe that life continues from one existence to another and the actions (kamma) in one existence influence the way life continues in a second existence.

This can be explained like the lighting of a candle from another. When the second candle is lit, it appears to have a new flame, and yet is a continuation of the flame from the first candle.

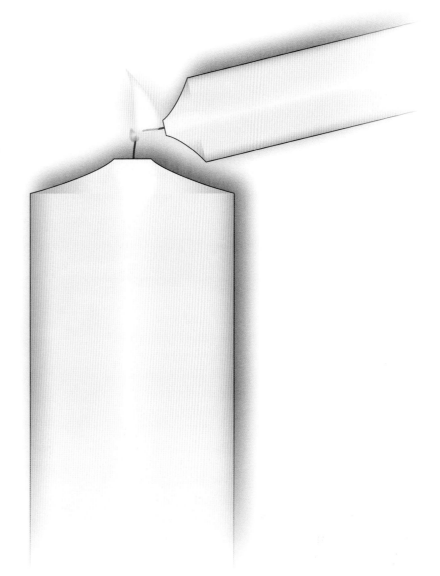

Nibbana

Nibbana is achieved when greed, anger and ignorance have been overcome. The Buddha said, 'nibbana is the greatest joy.'

Nibbana is the extinguishing (blowing out) of desire. It leads to a state of perfect peace. It may or may not lead to escaping samsara. The Buddha attained nibbana in his lifetime.

There are many different understandings about what nibbana means but all Buddhists are aware that death is inevitable and how a person behaves will affect what happens after a person dies.

Buddhist beliefs about life

Here are some quotations about life and the nature of life:

All wrong-doing arises because of mind. If mind is transformed can wrong-doing remain?

(The Buddha)

However many holy words you read, however many you speak, what good will they do you if you do not act upon them?

(The Buddha)

All beings have lived and died and been reborn countless times. Over and over again they have experienced the indescribable Clear Light. But because they are obscured by the darkness of ignorance, they wander endlessly in a limitless samsara.

(Padmasambhava)

There are those who do not realise that one day we all must die.

But those who do realise this settle their quarrels.

(The Buddha – Dhammapada)

I will not remain in this world any longer, but will go to dwell in the stronghold of the great bliss of deathlessness.

(The Last Testament of Longchenpa)

Tomorrow or the next life – which comes first, we never know.

(Tibetan saying)

Knowledge check

1 What did the Buddha teach about the nature of life?
2 What is samsara?
3 What is kamma? How does a Buddhist make good kamma?
4 What is nibbana?
5 How did the Buddha describe nibbana?

A Buddhist might say that Buddhist beliefs about the nature of life are important because they greatly affect the way people choose to live.

- A person's actions on Earth are important: good actions lead to **merit**, bad actions lead to lack of merit and are bad kamma.
- Buddhists will **meditate** so that they achieve a positive spiritual state.
- Buddhists will try to follow the teachings of the Buddha and the **Middle Way** – with no extremes.
- Buddhist beliefs about the nature of life give Buddhists an overall purpose to their life – to escape from suffering that is a natural part of life, to overcome suffering and experience true happiness.

Activity A

1 Draw an outline of the human body.

2 Inside the body write words that describe the things that a Buddhist who wishes to escape samsara and enter nibbana should try to do.

Activity B

In small groups design a board game showing a Buddhist's path to escaping samsara.

1 This could be based on snakes and ladders or a more complex Monopoly-type game with chance cards.

2 Play all the games in your class and decide which game is the best one.

Activity C

1 Read the quotations on page 28 and think about what Buddhists believe they say about life.

2 For each quotation, explain what it is saying.

3 Explain whether you agree with any of the quotations and why.

Activity D

1 In small groups make a list of all the reasons why you think belief in life after death is important, and another list stating why you think that belief in life after death is unimportant.

2 Hold a debate in the class and decide whether it is important to believe in life after death or not.

Learning objectives

You will ... • learn what Buddhism teaches about suffering

• understand how Buddhists respond to the problem of suffering

• learn about how Buddhists might react to different situations of suffering.

The Four Noble Truths

The **Four Noble Truths** are a central part of the Buddha's teaching. They are about the nature of suffering and how it can be overcome.

The Four Noble Truths are:

Life involves suffering (**dukkha**).

Suffering comes from attachment, craving and wanting things (**samudaya**).

Suffering can be overcome by ending craving (**nirodha** – unmaking attachments).

The way to end suffering is to follow the **Noble Eightfold Path** (**magga** – the Middle Way).

Buddhists would say this means:
- Suffering is part of life and is inevitable. It means a lack of satisfaction in how life is. A Buddhist might say that a person can be aware of this even when they are happy.
- We suffer because we want things to make us happy. But these same things can make us unhappy.
- Suffering does not have to continue once it has been recognised; it can be treated.
- The way to overcome suffering is to follow the principles laid out by the Buddha in the Noble Eightfold Path. It is a life without extremes: the Middle Way.

The things that make us happy can also cause us suffering.

Knowledge check

1 What are the Four Noble Truths?

2 What do Buddhists hope they will achieve by recognising the Four Noble Truths?

3 How is suffering caused according to Buddhist teachings?

4 How can suffering be overcome according to Buddhist teachings?

The Buddhist response to the problems caused by suffering

There are many ways that Buddhists respond to the problem of suffering.

Follow the Noble Eightfold Path

Avoid extremes of pleasure and hardship

Give money to charity

May accept that it is the result of negative kamma

Responses to suffering

Accept that suffering is natural and a part of life

Develop compassion towards others

Meditate, especially on **metta** (loving-kindness) to others

Keep to the rules (the **Five Precepts**) of not killing, not stealing, not being uncontrolled in lust, false speech, and not becoming intoxicated

Take up caring jobs

Activity A

1 Look at the responses to suffering given in the spidergram. Discuss them with a classmate.

2 Make a list of the responses you agree with. Add any responses to suffering that you have thought of in discussion with your classmate.

3 Explain in one paragraph how a Buddhist would address the problems caused by suffering.

Activity B

1 Using newspapers or news websites such as www.bbc.co.uk, find an example of suffering in the world today. Try to answer the following questions about the event (disaster):

- What caused it?
- Could it have been avoided?
- How are people reacting to it?
- How might Buddhists react to it?

2 In groups, design a poster/leaflet campaign to explain in Buddhist terms what caused the suffering and what Buddhists could do about it.

Activity C

Some people think that suffering is a part of life that affects everyone, and they should follow the Noble Eightfold Path to overcome attachment and suffering.

1 What three arguments could you give to support this point of view?

2 What three arguments could you give to disagree with this point of view?

Activity D

Plan and perform a role play about suffering.

1 Choose a situation that shows suffering. This can be a real event from the news or a fictional one.

2 Think about the characters in your role play. How do they react to suffering? Will they accept it, be angry, meditate or blame kamma?

3 Your role play should include a discussion about the Four Noble Truths as an explanation for this suffering and how Buddhists should respond to it.

2.3 What is the Noble Eightfold Path?

Learning objectives

You will ... • learn what the Noble Eightfold Path is
• describe the Noble Eightfold Path
• understand why the Noble Eightfold Path is important to Buddhists.

The Buddha taught that when people avoid the extremes of luxuries or hardships, and they live in a way that brings knowledge and wisdom, then they are following the Middle Way. In this way, they can overcome suffering.

In order to follow the Middle Way, Buddhists need to avoid extreme lifestyles and try to carry out the actions that are described as the Noble Eightfold Path.

For Buddhists, the Noble Eightfold Path is the right way to live. The Noble Eightfold Path is not a list of rules that has to be followed in a particular order. It contains eight principles that can be applied to everyday life (see diagram on page 33). The Noble Eightfold Path is the way that Buddhists believe they can overcome desire and suffering, so that they achieve **enlightenment**.

The principles of the Noble Eightfold Path can be divided into three categories:
- Morality (Sila) – this comprises of Right Action, Right Speech and Right Livelihood. Morality means that Buddhists will act in a morally correct way; they will behave well.
- Concentration (Samadhi) – this comprises of Right Effort, Right Concentration and Right Mindfulness. This is concentration so that the mind becomes alert; Buddhists will meditate to increase awareness.
- Wisdom (Panna) – this comprises of Right View and Right Intention. It means that the person is fully able to understand the nature of things.

Knowledge check

1 Where did the Noble Eightfold Path come from?

2 What is the Noble Eightfold Path?

3 Why would a Buddhist want to use the Noble Eightfold Path?

4 Do Buddhists have to follow the Noble Eightfold Path in a particular order? Give reasons for your answer.

5 Make a list of the eight principles that are included in the Noble Eightfold Path.

The Noble Eightfold Path

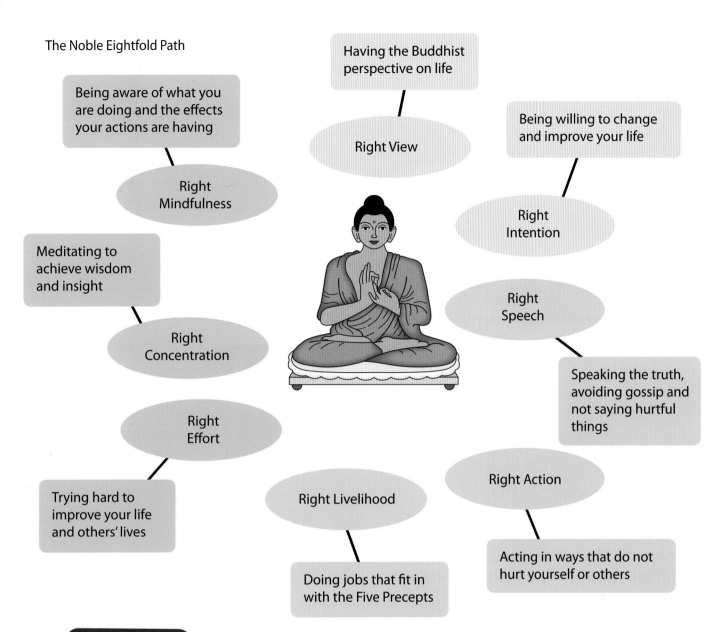

Having the Buddhist perspective on life

Being aware of what you are doing and the effects your actions are having

Being willing to change and improve your life

Right View

Right Mindfulness

Right Intention

Meditating to achieve wisdom and insight

Right Speech

Right Concentration

Speaking the truth, avoiding gossip and not saying hurtful things

Right Effort

Right Action

Trying hard to improve your life and others' lives

Right Livelihood

Acting in ways that do not hurt yourself or others

Doing jobs that fit in with the Five Precepts

Activity A

Using the glossary and the Noble Eightfold Path diagram above, copy and complete the table describing what the different parts of the Noble Eightfold Path mean.

Part of the Noble Eightfold Path	What it means
Right View	
Right Intention	
Right Speech	
Right Action	
Right Livelihood	
Right Effort	
Right Concentration	
Right Mindfulness	

Living the Noble Eightfold Path

Buddhists describe how the Noble Eightfold Path affects their lives.

I try to find out more about the teachings of the Buddha so I have the correct understanding of how to live.

It reminds me that I should be trying hard to improve others' lives as well as my own.

It means that when I meditate I am following the path to enlightenment.

I try not to say anything unless it is meaningful.

The path guides me when I think about what is the best occupation for me to follow.

Activity B

1 Read through the speech bubbles that describe how Buddhists have said the Noble Eightfold Path affects their lives. What questions would you ask each Buddhist about how the Path affects them?

2 Which principle would be the easiest to follow? Give reasons for your opinion.

3 Which principle would be the most difficult to follow? Give reasons for your opinion.

There have been many images of the Noble Eightfold Path produced throughout history to try to explain what the Noble Eightfold Path is and help Buddhists in the practice of the Path. Many are based on an eight-spoked wheel.

Activity C

1 In a group, choose one teaching from the Noble Eightfold Path that you think most affects the life of a Buddhist.

2 Write down at least three reasons why you think this teaching will affect a person's life the most.

3 Explain the decision your group made to the rest of the class in a brief presentation.

Activity D

1 Find some more images or symbols of the Noble Eightfold Path. You could look in books or search the Internet. Type 'Noble Eightfold Path' in a search engine and click the 'images' option.

2 Investigate when these images were created, by whom and why.

3 Make a display using the pictures and include explanations of what each picture shows about the Noble Eightfold Path.

Learning objectives

You will ...
- learn what the Wheel of Life is
- understand why the Wheel of Life is important for some Buddhists
- analyse images of the Wheel of Life.

The Wheel of Life (**Bhavacakka**) is a symbol that is used by Tibetan Buddhists to summarise Buddhist teachings about the meaning of existence. It shows the cycle of samsara:

- life
- death, and
- rebirth.

The wheel shows things that happen in life and how a person's choices and behaviour affect their future.

The wheel is held by Yama, the Lord of Death and Change, showing that death has control of the entire wheel. (Death controls when life changes because death is the cause of rebirth.) The inside of the wheel is divided into six realms or worlds. These are states of mind that people move between in their daily lives: misery, anger, greed, happiness and so on.

The centre of the wheel illustrates a pig, a snake and a cockerel – these symbolise the **Three Poisons**: greed, anger and ignorance. The Three Poisons are those things that Buddhists believe keep all beings trapped in samsara; they are the centre of the wheel as they show that everything revolves around them. The Three Poisons create kamma: they are shown on the Wheel of Life as animals holding on to each other's tails to show they are linked to each other. For example, greed is often a result of ignorance and ignorance often causes anger.

Knowledge check

1 What is the Wheel of Life?
2 What does the Wheel of Life symbolise?
3 What is shown on the outside of the wheel? Give reasons why.
4 What do the inside of the wheel's six areas symbolise?
5 What animals are shown in the centre of the wheel?
6 What do the animals in the centre of the wheel symbolise?

Activity A

1 Draw and label symbols (other than a snake, cockerel or pig) to show the Three Poisons.
2 In the wheel these animals hold one another's tails to show they are interlinked. Try to show in your symbols how they link.
3 Discuss your symbols and decide what is good about them.

Buddhists show their beliefs about life and teachings about the meaning of existence in pictures like this one called *The Wheel of Life*.

The six realms of the Wheel of Life

Realm	What it shows	Modern examples
Realm of the Gods	• People living in this realm have happiness, wealth and contentment. • The problem with this is they do not strive to make things better or look after those who suffer.	Wealthy people constantly on holiday and who never work.
Realm of the Jealous Gods	• People living here are ambitious power seekers. • They are envious of others. • On the other hand, ambitious, powerful people can achieve great changes in the world.	Some politicians and corporate leaders.
Animal Realm	• People who are dominated by their basic animal instincts, ignoring their spiritual side. • They do not care about others and are always trying to put them down. • They are very self-centred, caring only about their personal wellbeing.	People who think only about food, possessions or how they look.
Hell Realm	• People who are angry and aggressive (in fire) and people who show no feeling (in ice) – caused by anger, greed and ignorance. • People who suffer from misery and depression.	People who are abusive or those who purposely isolate themselves.
Realm of the Hungry Ghosts	• People who are greedy and addicted to things so they always want more. • People who are unable to look any further than their own needs.	People who have enough but always want more.
Human Realm	• Those people who choose to follow the Buddha's teaching. People are able to reach enlightenment from this realm. • But most people spend time seeking pleasure and avoiding suffering.	People caught up in the day-to-day concerns of life. Also people who have chosen to follow the **Dhamma**.

Activity B

1 You have been asked to design and paint a mural of the Wheel of Life for a wall on the side of a vihara. The mural has to be purely symbolic, making use of images and words.

2 Plan and draw a picture of the mural.

3 Include with your mural an explanation of what you like about the mural and what different Buddhists might think of it.

Activity C

1 Read the table on page 38 carefully. Think about the types of people that would be found in each realm. Choose one of the realms and think of an example of someone who might be found in this realm, for example a person addicted to computer games might be in the realm of hungry ghosts.

2 In pairs, describe your example and explain why they are in the realm you have chosen.

3 Write a letter to the person in your example, giving them advice about how they should live according to Buddhist teachings.

Activity D

1 Produce a set of posters or a PowerPoint presentation to explain the Buddhist teaching on the Wheel of Life to members of other faiths. You should include:

a a description of the Wheel of Life
b explanations of what the Wheel of Life symbolises
c explanations of why Buddhists use the Wheel of Life
d some chosen images of the Wheel of Life.

2 You must do some research and provide an explanation to accompany your set of posters or PowerPoint presentation.

2.5 What is enlightenment?

Learning objectives

You will ...
- identify beliefs that Buddhists have about enlightenment
- learn what enlightenment is
- understand the importance of enlightenment for Buddhists.

A Buddha is a person who is enlightened.

The greatest gift is to give people your enlightenment.
(The Buddha)

The whole secret of existence is to have no fear.
(The Buddha)

Do not think you will necessarily be aware of your own enlightenment
(Dogen – Buddhist monk)

Enlightenment is an end to suffering.

Enlightenment is awakening to a reality most people never notice.

Enlightenment

Enlightenment is permanent because we have not produced it; we have merely discovered it.
(Chogyam Trungpa – Buddhist meditation teacher)

Enlightenment is when a person has achieved supreme wisdom and spiritual understanding or insight.

Enlightenment is freedom from attachments to worldly things.

Keep yourself straight and clear and be a happy human being today.
If you keep your situation happy day by day, you will eventually reach the greatest happiness of enlightenment
(Lama Yeshe – Tibetan monk)

Knowledge check

1. What does 'enlightenment' mean?
2. Look at the quotations in the spidergram above. Make a list of all the words that can be used to describe enlightenment.
3. Using the glossary and a dictionary, write down what these words mean.

Activity A

1. Produce an advertising poster to encourage people to seek enlightenment.
2. Include in your poster a headline, a picture and a description of what enlightenment is supposed to be like.

Describing enlightenment

Here are some words that are used to describe enlightenment:

Awake

Happy

Clear

Permanent

Powerful

Spontaneous

Great

Intense

Conscious

Indescribable

Spiritual

Freedom

Activity B

1 Look at the words used to describe enlightenment. Choose two of them, and for each word:

   a write down at least three reasons why you think the word is a good word to use when describing enlightenment

   b then write down at least three reasons why you think the word is not a good word to use when describing enlightenment.

2 Can you think of any other words that describe enlightenment?

3 Think about the way that these words can be symbolised in pictures, for example, power is symbolised as fire or wind, happy is symbolised with a smile or smiley face, and so on. Draw a symbol for the word that you think describes enlightenment well.

Activity C

In small groups, role play a TV panel interview with a **Bodhisatta** (a person who is an enlightened being and who has put off entering nibbana to help others).

1 Write down at least five interview questions. One of the questions should ask how he/she feels about some of the words that are used to describe enlightenment.

2 Another question should ask about how enlightenment can be achieved.

3 Another question should ask what difference enlightenment should make for a person.

4 How do you think an enlightened being would answer these questions? Do you think they would want to boast about being enlightened?

Activity D

We are perfect, we all have Buddha nature, but we haven't yet realised it.
(Reverend Sarika Dhamma)

Read the quotation from Sarika Dhamma and think about what she wanted the reader to understand about enlightenment.

1 What does the quotation tell you about her view of enlightenment?

2 What does the quotation tell you about the way she thinks enlightenment is achieved?

3 What does the quotation tell you about her feelings towards other people?

4 How might her view of enlightenment have affected her life?

5 Do you have the same view of enlightenment as Sarika Dhamma? Explain your reasons.

2.6 Why are there different groups of Buddhists?

Learning objectives

You will ...
- learn about the different groups of Buddhists
- understand what the different groups of Buddhists believe
- explain why there are different groups of Buddhists.

There are around 376 million Buddhists all around the world and more than 150,000 of them live in Great Britain. They all share common beliefs about the nature and purpose of life, based on the teachings of Siddattha Gotama.

Many different Buddhist groups have developed in different parts of the world that Buddhists live. They have been influenced by the people around them, the cultures they live in and existing faiths. The different groups place different amounts of importance on different Buddhist teachings and methods of **worship**.

The three main different groups are **Theravada**, **Mahayana** and Tibetan Buddhism. There are also contemporary groups that have formed more recently, which adapt Buddhism to modern life.

Knowledge check

1. How many Buddhists are there in the world?
2. How many Buddhists live in Great Britain?
3. What beliefs do all Buddhists share?
4. Give two reasons why there are different Buddhist groups.
5. Name four Buddhist groups.
6. Where did Theravada Buddhism develop?
7. What is another name given to Mahayana Buddhism?
8. What is Tibetan Buddhism like?
9. What are contemporary Buddhist groups? Name one.

Theravada means 'tradition of the elders' and it dates back to early Buddhism, which developed in India. It is now mainly found in Thailand, Sri Lanka and Burma.	Mahayanan Buddhism is often called The Great Vehicle and includes a number of different types of Buddhism. It developed in India and is popular in the Far East.	Tibetan Buddhism developed from the Mahayana tradition and mixed with folk religion. It is a lively and colourful form of Buddhism.	A well known modern group is the Triratna Buddhist Order, formerly Friends of the Western Buddhist Order. It started in London in 1968 and follows a mixture of different Buddhist ideas.

Why are there different Buddhist groups?

Some Buddhists wish to live in ways that concentrate on the spiritual side of life.

Buddhism can vary from country to country.

Some Buddhists wish to concentrate on different teachings than other Buddhists.

Why are there different Buddhist groups?

Buddhism varies according to the culture of the country.

So that Buddhism is relevant to different types of people.

Some Buddhists wish to follow a more traditional form of Buddhism.

To allow people to practise a form of Buddhism that most suits them.

Activity A

1   Make a list of the similarities between the different Buddhists.

2   Make a list of the differences that you can see between the Buddhists from the different groups.

Activity B

Look at the spidergram above. There are many reasons why there are different Buddhist groups.

1   Can you think of any more reasons why there may be many different Buddhist groups?

2   What are the advantages of having lots of different Buddhist groups? Give reasons for your answer.

3   What are the disadvantages of having lots of different Buddhist groups? Give reasons for your answer.

Activity C

1   Design a booklet for a Year 6 pupil to explain some of the similarities and differences between Buddhist groups, and to explain why there are differences. You could refer to:

   • the similarities in basic beliefs
   • the different scriptures used
   • the differences in aim of life
   • methods of worship.

2   In groups, analyse your booklets and decide which one best explains the differences between the Buddhist groups.

Activity D

Mahayanan Buddhists use a lot of rituals in the practice of their religion. They have death rituals where they make offerings of flowers, chant using prayer beads and burn incense. Theravadin Buddhists do not do this to the same extent.

1   Do you think these different practices mean that Buddhists are not following the same religion?

2   Do you think these different practices help or confuse people? Give reasons for your answer.

3   Find out more about the differences between the other groups of Buddhists, especially the Triratna Buddhist Order. Why do you think this group of Buddhists usually wears western clothes?

The big assignment

Task

To produce a newspaper summarising Buddhist beliefs.

Objectives

- To research a number of topics to give an overview of the main Buddhist beliefs.

- To find and use material from Buddhist scriptures, religious leaders and the media that can provide evidence for your newspaper.

Outcome

To produce a newspaper that could be used by Buddhists to give information to people of other religions about the main beliefs of Buddhism.

You should include information about:

- the nature of life

- the Four Noble Truths

- enlightenment.

Guidance

1 Work in groups of six or seven people. Each person should be given a specific job to do, and the rest of the group should support them in doing it.

2 Suggested jobs:

  a Researching what kinds of beliefs people would like to find out about in a newspaper. What types of people would read this kind of newspaper? Why?

  b Writing questions to ask Buddhists to help you find out about their beliefs.

  c Interviewing Buddhists to help you find out about their beliefs.

  d Asking the questions and writing up the answers.

  e Finding out evidence of Buddhist teachings about topics through Internet-based research and library research.

  f Taking photographs or finding relevant illustrations to go with the information.

  g Planning the layout of the newspaper to ensure that sufficient space is given to the various pieces of information.

3 As a group, go through the material gathered, i.e. the outcomes of each job, and for each one decide what needs to be done to finish it.

4 Remember to include an editor's comment in the newspaper to explain why the particular beliefs have been investigated.

5 Your completed newspaper should contain photographs, diagrams, text, summaries and links to evidence that can be found in books, on the Internet, in the interviews you have written or filmed, and so on.

6 Present your newspaper to a Buddhist, and ask for feedback.

7 As a group, evaluate your newspaper: decide what you did well and what you could have improved.

Assessment

You will be assessed on:

✓ how well you use specialist vocabulary

✓ your ability to explain the religious beliefs

✓ your ability to explain how important the beliefs are to Buddhists

✓ how well organised your newspaper is

✓ how you allocated roles, and how well you worked with others

✓ your evaluation of the success of your team.

3.1 How do Buddhists make moral decisions?

Learning objectives

You will ...
- learn what an ethical decision is
- understand how Buddhists make ethical decisions
- explain how a Buddhist would answer particular moral problems.

Ethics is the study of what is right and what is wrong; what is good and what is bad.

Our ethics are often called morals.

Justice is based on what is ethically right.

What a person regards as ethical will have an effect on all the decisions they make in their life.

ETHICAL DECISIONS

Buddhist ethics recognise that the motivation for an action is important. A Buddhist works out why they want to do something and then considers its effects before doing anything.

Different people have different views about what is ethically or morally acceptable or right.

There are different ethical ideas that people use to make moral decisions.
Making ethical or moral decisions is often very difficult as the answers are not obvious.

Activity A

1 Think about a decision you have made recently. Try to answer the following questions:

- Was it an easy decision to make?
- Was it an important decision?
- Did you ask anyone's advice? Why?
- Were you happy with the outcome of your decision? Why?

2 Do you think very important decisions are more or less easy to make than other decisions? Can you think of any reasons why this is the case?

Knowledge check

1 What are morals?

2 What is an ethical decision?

3 Are ethical decisions easy to make? Why?

4 Why do ethics affect the decisions a person has to make?

5 What is important about Buddhist ethics?

We have already discovered that there are different groups of Buddhists, and within each group there are individuals who hold different views on how decisions should be made. Buddhists do not recognise any rules that must be stuck to and not broken when making decisions. Each decision will be made on its own particular strengths and weaknesses. Buddhists will, however, consider various factors when making a decision (see boxes on page 47).

Dhamma

- These are the natural laws about life that were recognised by the Buddha.
- These laws organise and underpin the universe.
- **Dhamma** gives regularity to the way the world works.
- If a person lives according to Dhamma they will be acting morally.

Teachings of the Buddha (Buddha Dhamma)

- The **Buddha** had authority to help guide others.
- The Buddha's teachings can guide people to reach enlightenment.
- The Buddha's teachings provide moral guidelines to live by.

Activity B

1   Discuss the following with a classmate. What would you advise?

    A Buddhist has to decide between:

    - telling the truth and hurting someone's feelings; or
    - keeping quiet and keeping the person happy.

2   Think about how the Buddhist would use different sources of guidance to help. Would the different sources in the boxes above give the same advice? Why?

3   What do you think the Buddhist should do: tell the truth or lie?

Activity D

In small groups, produce a problem advice page for young Buddhists. You should try to include:

- at least three different moral dilemmas
- what advice you would give – taken from the different sources of advice above
- a reply from one of the letter writers saying what the outcome of the decision was.

Kammic action

- It determines whether an action will bring **merit** (good **kamma**).
- It can provide a motivation to act in a certain way.
- If a decision is a personal one it needs an individual's own response.

The Five Precepts

The **Five Precepts** are guides for Buddhist life. They are:

- not killing,
- not stealing,
- not being uncontrolled in lust,
- not using false speech (lying),
- not becoming **intoxicated**.

The moral decision a Buddhist decides to take should follow the Precepts as they are for the benefit of everyone, not just the person following them.

Precepts can be easily applied to many moral decisions. For example, not using false speech means that a Buddhist should tell the truth, although if someone asks them about something that is very personal this can be difficult because Buddhists try to avoid causing suffering by upsetting anyone.

Activity C

1   Write a booklet for an 11–12 year-old Buddhist child, explaining how they should make decisions. You should include:

    - what a moral decision is
    - the four guiding factors that need to be considered
    - an example of a moral decision (e.g. cheating in an exam).

2   In groups, analyse your booklets and decide which one your group thinks is the best at explaining how to make moral decisions.

Learning objectives

You will …
- learn what human rights are
- understand Buddhist teachings about human rights
- assess a particular human rights situation and judge how Buddhists could react to it.

Human rights are those rights or entitlements that everyone has simply because they are human beings. They are so important that the United Nations produced a list of the human rights that people are entitled to. It is called the Universal Declaration of Human Rights. The legal systems of most countries are made in order to protect people's rights.

Human rights include:

1 We are all **born free**. We should all be treated in the same way.
2 These rights **belong to everybody**, whatever they think or whatever they believe.
3 We all have the right to life, and to live in **freedom** and **safety**.
4 Nobody has any right to make us a slave.
5 Nobody has any right to hurt us or to torture us.
6 The law is the **same** for everyone.
7 Nobody has the right to put us in prison without a good reason.
8 If we are frightened of being badly treated in our own country, we all have the **right to run away** to another country to be safe.
9 Every grown-up has the **right to marry** and have a **family** if they want to.
10 Everyone has the **right to own things**.
11 We all have the right to believe in what we want to.
12 We all have the **right to think** and **say what we like**.

ALL HUMAN BEINGS ARE BORN FREE AND EQUAL IN DIGNITY AND RIGHTS. THEY ARE ENDOWED WITH REASON AND CONSCIENCE AND SHOULD ACT TOWARDS ONE ANOTHER IN A SPIRIT OF BROTHERHOOD.

Knowledge check

1 What is a human right?
2 Who is allowed human rights?
3 Who produced a declaration of human rights that countries should agree to?
4 How does each country protect people's human rights?
5 Name three rights that human beings are entitled to.
6 Why do you think human rights are important?

Human rights as an idea is relatively modern and not one that can be found in the teachings of the Buddha, but the underlying concept is one that can be found within Buddhism.

Buddhists have a duty to care for others.

All Buddhists should show compassion towards others.

Supporting others' rights will lead to good merit (good kamma).

Buddhist teachings supporting human rights

All individuals are equal.

The first two Five Precepts support basic human rights.

Avoiding the **Three Poisons** means supporting others' rights.

Activity A

1 Read the human rights listed on page 48. You could also look for a summary of all human rights on the Internet, using www.un.org or www.humanrights.com. Discuss the rights with a classmate. Which do you think are the most important?

2 With your classmate, make a list or draw a concept map of all the human rights that are important to you – they do not all have to come from the list given on page 48.

3 If you had to decide on one human right being the most important, which would you choose? Why?

4 Do you think it is important that all countries accept the same list of human rights? Why?

Activity B

Part of the work of the Buddhist charity Tzu Chi Foundation is to stand up for human rights. They state on their website that their mission focuses on giving material aid to the needy and inspiring love and humanity in all. The foundation also dedicates itself in the fields of medicine, education, environmental protection, international relief work and the establishment of a marrow donor registry. Through helping those in need, Tzu Chi volunteers take on **Bodhisatta** practices, the way to Buddhahood (**enlightenment**).

1 Why do you think the foundation does this work?

2 The foundation helped the survivors of the 2011 Japanese earthquake, providing food and blankets. Which human rights do you think this is supporting?

3 What three reasons could a Buddhist give for supporting this work?

Activity C

1 Using newspaper articles or a website such as Amnesty International (www.amnesty.org.uk), find an example of abuse of human rights in the world today. Find out:

- What caused it?
- Could it have been avoided?
- How are people reacting to it?
- How might a Buddhist react?

2 In groups, design a poster/leaflet campaign to explain what is happening in the example you have chosen and what Buddhists could do about it.

Activity D

Plan and perform a role play about human rights.

1 Research a situation in the world where human rights are being ignored.

2 Organise characters for a role play. Include people whose rights are ignored, people abusing human rights, charity workers and a Buddhist.

3 Include a discussion in the role play of whether human rights have been abused and how a Buddhist might respond to the situation.

Learning objectives

You will ... • understand the terms animal rights, metta and vegetarian
• understand and analyse Buddhist attitudes to animal rights and vegetarianism.

Animal rights

Animal rights can mean many things, but it always means that animals have the right not to be harmed or exploited (taken advantage of) by humans and it sometimes means that animals should be given the same consideration as humans.

Most Buddhists will treat animals with care and try to protect animal rights.

Buddhists try to show **metta** (loving-kindness) to all, and this includes animals. They may **meditate** to let love flow through the universe to animals, and they cannot do this and ignore animal rights at the same time.

Buddhists try to develop compassion to all living beings, including animals.

The arhats (those who are free from the Three Poisons), who do not harm others and are always restrained in their actions, go to the deathless nibbana, where there is no sorrow.

(Dhammapada 225)

Why Buddhists try to protect animal rights

Not to revile, not to do any harm, to practise restraint according to the Fundamental Instructions for the bhikkhus, to be moderate in taking food, to dwell in a secluded place, to devote oneself to higher concentration – this is the Teaching of the Buddha.

(Dhammapada 185)

Knowledge check

1 What does the phrase 'animal rights' mean?

2 What is metta?

3 How might Buddhists show metta to animals?

4 According to the Dalai Lama, how can animals contribute to the world?

All beings possess Buddha nature, so all beings, including animals, are able to be enlightened if or when they are reborn as human beings.

One of the precepts is to do no harm. Although life does not end – it changes – Buddhists try not to kill as this is not a loving action.

All beings fear before danger; life is dear to all. When a man considers this, he does not kill or cause to kill.
(Dhammapada 129 and 130)

The creatures that inhabit this Earth – be they human beings or animals – are here to contribute, each in its own particular way, to the beauty and prosperity of the world.
(The 14th Dalai Lama, Tenzin Gyatso)

Vegetarianism

Although most **Theravadin** Buddhists are vegetarian, most **Mahayanan** Buddhists are not. Some Buddhists will eat meat only if that is what they are offered to eat, but if they are preparing their own food it will be vegetarian. This is because even though the Buddha encouraged his followers not to harm living things, he also described circumstances when eating meat was acceptable. Some scriptures show that he ate meat himself, whereas other scriptures recall him telling followers not to eat meat.

Here is a table showing Buddhist attitudes to animal rights and vegetarianism.

	Some Buddhists believe	Other Buddhists believe
Animal rights	All **sentient** beings should support each other. All living beings have the possibility of enlightenment. Buddhists should show metta to all living beings.	Bad kamma can result in rebirth as an animal. The teachings in Buddhist scriptures refer to respect for humans more than animals. Animals are different from human beings.
Vegetarianism	Killing is against one of the Five Precepts. Killing causes suffering, which should be avoided if possible. Killing may result in negative kamma. Animals are part of the cycle of **samsara** and by interfering with animal life you are affecting their chances of achieving a good rebirth.	Eating meat is acceptable because everything is impermanent and subject to change. The Buddha is recorded as eating meat. It is acceptable to eat meat that has been provided by others, but not to kill or harm animals.

Activity A

1 Design a questionnaire that you could give to people to find out their opinions about whether they think animals should have the same rights as human beings, similar rights to human beings, or whether some rights should be different for humans and animals.

2 If possible, ask people to complete your questionnaire, then evaluate what you find out.

Activity B

Look at the Buddhist views about animal rights and vegetarianism in the table above. Discuss and answer these questions:

1 Which view about animal rights do you agree with?

2 Give reasons for your answer.

3 Which view about vegetarianism do you agree with?

4 Give reasons for your answer.

1 In small groups, choose either animal rights or vegetarianism.

2 Make a concept map of all of the opinions about the topic that your group has.

3 Include on the concept map all the different reasons why the group has these views.

4 Design a poster to show all the different opinions that people have and why they have them.

5 Explain your poster to the rest of the class.

Activity D

Animal rights **activists** appear in newspaper articles because they have very strong opinions about how people care for animals. They have on occasion tried to free animals from captivity. Try to find an example of a newspaper article about animal rights or an organisation that works for animal rights and that is supported by Buddhists.

1 Write a newspaper article for a Buddhist magazine about animal rights.

2 Include:

• the different main opinions about the issue and why people hold them

• quotations and examples for the different opinions that Buddhists might have.

3.4 What does Buddhism teach about environmental issues?

Learning objectives

You will ...
- learn about the issues surrounding the environment
- understand and analyse Buddhist attitudes to the environment.

Environmental issues are those that affect the natural world and everything that lives in it. They affect everyone in some way. Issues include **climate change**, preservation of wildlife, **pollution**, use of natural resources and why people should try to live in ways that do not harm the environment.

Environmental issues are important to Buddhists because of their teachings and beliefs about the Earth and looking after it. The main Buddhist concepts connected to environmental issues are:

All life is interlinked so Buddhists should take care of all of it.

Taking life is wrong as it is one of the Five Precepts – this includes animal life.

Change is inevitable. However, Buddhists try to avoid suffering at the same time as accepting change.

Humans are responsible for caring for the Earth. This is part of the teachings about **compassion** and loving kindness.

The Jataka Tales (part of the **Tipitaka**) makes no distinction between animals and humans – all display the same feelings and emotions.
Some of the tales describe the Buddha's previous lives in the form of animals.

People should try to live in harmony with nature.

Buddhists try to gain merit from their actions (good kamma) and so will help the environment.

Knowledge check

1 What does 'environmental issue' mean?

2 Give two examples of environmental issues.

3 Give three reasons why Buddhists might think that they should look after the world and everything in it.

Buddhists believe that humans are responsible for caring for the Earth. This is part of the Buddhist teachings about compassion and loving kindness.

Activity A

In groups produce a banner that could be displayed in a classroom to show Buddhist ideas about the environment. It should include:

- pictures
- Buddhist teachings
- descriptions of problems in the environment
- practical ways Buddhists can help the environment.

We need to live as the Buddha taught us to live, in peace and harmony with nature, but this must start with ourselves. If we are going to save this planet we need to seek a new ecological order, to look at the life we lead and then work together for the benefit of all; unless we work together no solution can be found. By moving away from self-centredness, sharing wealth more, being more responsible for ourselves, and agreeing to live more simply, we can help decrease much of the suffering in the world.

(Buddhist Statement on Ecology, 1996)

Activity B

1 Consider the reasons why Buddhists think environmental issues are important.

2 In pairs discuss the Buddhist Statement on Ecology. Decide whether you agree with all of the statement, then discuss why you agree or disagree.

3 Produce a single side of A4 handout, or design a computer pop-up that could be used to raise awareness of one current environmental issue and what a Buddhist might say about it.

Environmental issues

The issues surrounding care for the environment include ensuring that the world is kept in its natural state as far as possible, so taking care of the world for the future. The environment is suffering because of climate change and **global warming**, pollution and overuse of natural resources. Buddhists are active in trying to protect the environment. There are many Buddhist groups that are concerned with the environment, such as Earth Sangha, and Buddhism is one of ten religions that are part of the Alliance of Religions and Conservation group (ARC). You can find out more about ARC at www.arcworld.org.

Buddhists also try to help after environmental problems, whether they are natural, such as earthquakes and tsunamis, or man-made, such as oil spills or deforestation.

Buddhists work to raise awareness that everything we do on Earth will have a far-reaching effect.

They may practise Earth-healing meditation – focusing on healing the world.

They organise seed banks to save and grow seeds so they can be planted in areas where plants have been removed.

How Buddhists try to protect the environment

They try to develop compassion for all living beings.

They farm and grow crops in an environmentally-friendly way, and teach others to do the same.

Because of the precept not to cause harm, they try not to kill anything.

They raise awareness of the ways that humans are abusing the Earth and its resources. For example, some protest against timber harvesting.

Activity C

1 Organise a class debate: 'People should do more to protect the environment'.

2 The class should be divided in two: one half should prepare arguments in favour of the statement and the other half should prepare arguments against the statement. Both halves should include Buddhist arguments.

3 Choose a spokesperson to speak on behalf of each view and a chairperson to ensure that questions are asked in an orderly manner.

4 Each spokesperson should give a speech on the view and then the chairperson should allow the class to ask questions.

5 When all questions have been asked, the class should vote to see what the overall opinion of the class is.

Activity D

1 In groups, create a PowerPoint presentation on why Buddhists should care about the environment. Include in the presentation:

- descriptions of various ways Buddhists care for the environment
- pictures/photos
- Buddhist concepts
- various practical ways to help.

2 Your presentation could also include:

- appropriate music
- discussion about whether Buddhists should do anything at all because, if the world is natural, it should be left alone.

3.5 What does Buddhism teach about careers and employment?

Learning objectives

You will ...
- learn about the issues surrounding careers and acceptable types of employment
- understand and analyse Buddhist attitudes to certain types of employment.

Buddhist teaching about how to live means that some careers are not acceptable. Which ones?

A career is more than just the way that people earn money to live. It is often part of a person's way of life and, according to Buddhist values, should help them gain merit, reach self-fulfilment and understanding so that they can reach enlightenment.

Buddhist beliefs about careers and employment are all linked to the Five Precepts and the **Noble Eightfold Path**.

The Five Precepts mean that Buddhists should not undertake careers that lead to harm, taking what is not freely given, lying (false speech), sexual misconduct or involvement with intoxicating substances.

The Noble Eightfold Path includes elements that are essential for Buddhist understanding of what careers are acceptable. Obviously Right Livelihood would have to be considered, however, Right Speech, Right Action, Right Effort and Right Mindfulness will also influence what careers a Buddhist chooses to follow and how a Buddhist will behave in their career.

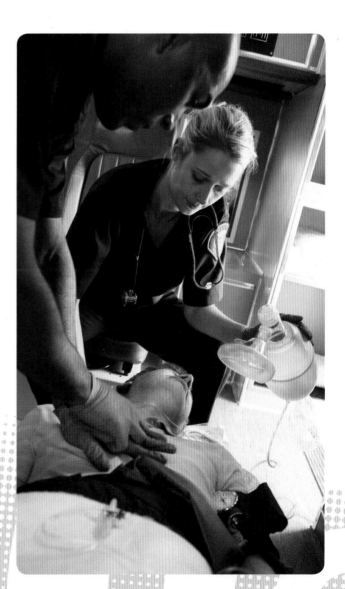

Knowledge check

1 What should a Buddhist's career do for them as well as provide them with money to live on?

2 Why is a Buddhist's career choice important?

3 What two main sets of teaching affect a Buddhist's choice of career?

4 Why are the Five Precepts important in a Buddhist's choice of career?

5 Why is the Noble Eightfold Path important in a Buddhist's choice of career?

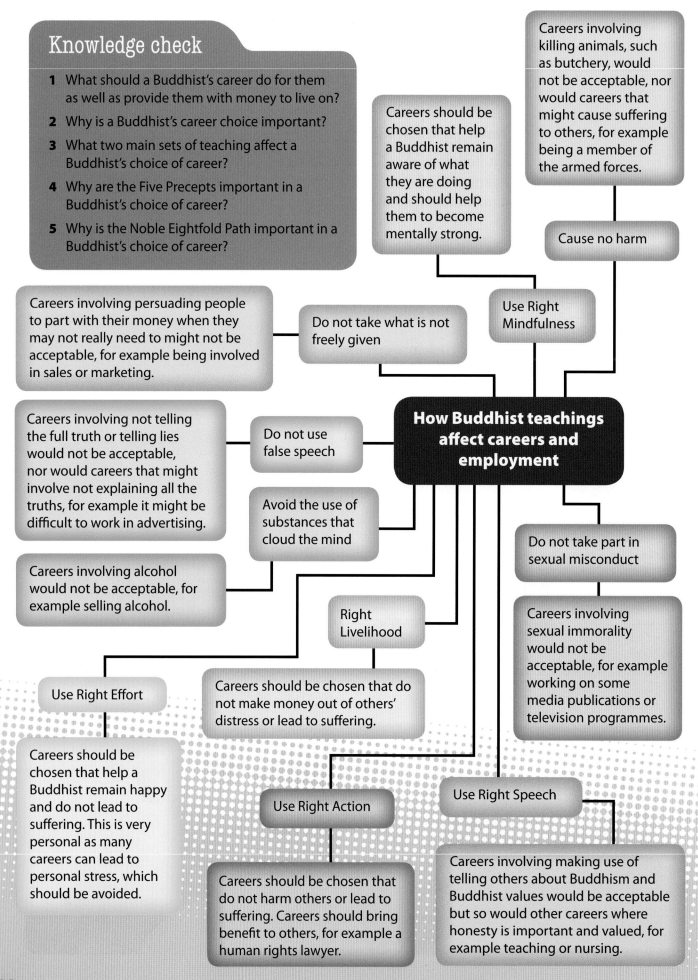

Careers involving killing animals, such as butchery, would not be acceptable, nor would careers that might cause suffering to others, for example being a member of the armed forces.

Careers should be chosen that help a Buddhist remain aware of what they are doing and should help them to become mentally strong.

Cause no harm

Use Right Mindfulness

Careers involving persuading people to part with their money when they may not really need to might not be acceptable, for example being involved in sales or marketing.

Do not take what is not freely given

How Buddhist teachings affect careers and employment

Careers involving not telling the full truth or telling lies would not be acceptable, nor would careers that might involve not explaining all the truths, for example it might be difficult to work in advertising.

Do not use false speech

Avoid the use of substances that cloud the mind

Do not take part in sexual misconduct

Careers involving alcohol would not be acceptable, for example selling alcohol.

Careers involving sexual immorality would not be acceptable, for example working on some media publications or television programmes.

Right Livelihood

Use Right Effort

Careers should be chosen that do not make money out of others' distress or lead to suffering.

Careers should be chosen that help a Buddhist remain happy and do not lead to suffering. This is very personal as many careers can lead to personal stress, which should be avoided.

Use Right Action

Use Right Speech

Careers should be chosen that do not harm others or lead to suffering. Careers should bring benefit to others, for example a human rights lawyer.

Careers involving making use of telling others about Buddhism and Buddhist values would be acceptable but so would other careers where honesty is important and valued, for example teaching or nursing.

Activity A

Copy the table below and complete it to show Buddhist teaching and how it might affect a Buddhist's choice of career.

Buddhist teaching	How it might affect a Buddhist's choice of career
Do not take what is not freely given	
Right Livelihood	
Right Mindfulness	
Right Effort	
Cause no harm	
Right Action	
Do not use false speech	
Avoid the use of substances which cloud the mind	

Activity B

1 In groups, produce a 'put yourself on the line' sheet. Draw a line across a large sheet of paper. At one end of the line write 'Buddhists can do any job that they want' and at the other end write 'Buddhists should never do any job that might go against Buddhist teaching'.

2 Take it in turns to mark on the line where you would put yourself.

3 Explain your reasons for where you placed yourself on the line.

Activity C

Mr X is a Buddhist who has four children and a home to run. He has just been offered a really well paid promotion to supermarket manager in charge of the fresh meat counter. He is now considering whether to take the job or leave the company.

1 In small groups, consider the case of Mr X.

2 What advice would you give Mr X? Why?

3 If Mr X was not a Buddhist, would your advice change? Why?

Activity D

Pupils should be divided into ten different groups. Each group should be allocated one of the Buddhist teachings that affect a Buddhist's choice about careers (see the spidergram on page 60). For each teaching:

• prepare a concept map to cover the issue, which can be taught to the rest of the class

• produce a fun quiz about the teaching and which careers it affects.

Learning objectives

You will ...
- identify different Buddhist attitudes to war and conflict
- understand why Buddhists have these attitudes towards war and conflict
- suggest how a Buddhist attitude to war and conflict could be supported.

Buddhist attitudes to war and peace

The main attitude Buddhists have towards conflict of any kind is that it is wrong. Buddhists try to live in peace with the world around them and recognise that any negative action towards another being will have far-reaching effects. The Five Precepts forbid causing harm to anything. They regard conflict as being unskilful (i.e. it will create negative effects) and believe that there must be peaceful ways to solve problems.

'Hatred does not cease by hatred at any time; by love alone does it cease.'

(Dhammapada)

There are instances, however, where Buddhists have been involved in conflict. The majority of these are justified as cases of self-defence.

Martial arts that have been developed by some monks (for example, Shaolin monks) have been used in conflicts, although the main aim of them is to practise self-discipline. The monks who practise them are forbidden to use them to inflict harm on others, or they can only fight in self-defence. In more modern cases, Buddhists have been involved in political protests that, although beginning peacefully, do not always end peacefully. Some Buddhists will say it is acceptable in some cases in order to protect the innocent from unnecessary suffering.

Originally developed as a form of self-defence, there are many different branches of martial arts being practised today. However, all of them require intense mental and physical discipline.

Why Buddhists might disagree with war and conflict

- It is against the precept not to cause harm.
- Many Buddhists consider conflict to be unskilful (it has negative effects).
- It is against the teachings of loving kindness and compassion.

Why Buddhists might agree with war and conflict

- It might protect innocent people from suffering.
- It can be used in self-defence.

Knowledge check

1 What are the main Buddhist attitudes to war and conflict?
2 What are the different attitudes all based on?
3 Why might Buddhists disagree with war and conflict?
4 Why might Buddhists agree with conflict?

Activity A

1 Imagine you are a journalist reporting for a Sunday morning TV programme. You are going to give a report on the attitudes that Buddhists have towards war and peace.

2 You need to explain the different Buddhist attitudes and the reasons for them. You might need to do some research and write down notes to help you.

3 Think about how to present your report in an entertaining but informative manner suitable for TV, before presenting it to the class.

Activity B

1 Draw a table with two columns. Call one column 'Why Buddhists might disagree with war and conflict', and the other 'Why Buddhists might agree with war and conflict'.

2 In each column record all the different reasons why you think different Buddhists might hold these views. Join with a classmate and then add any more reasons to your table. Then join with another pair and add any new ideas to your table.

3 On your own, answer the question: Why are there different attitudes to war and conflict among Buddhists?

One example of how Buddhists work to end conflict

Since 1962, there has been a conflict in Myanmar (also called Burma) between the military government and some people who want democracy and more freedom there.

In November 2011, five Buddhist monks were involved in protesting against the government in Myanmar. They wanted the government to release political prisoners. They put up posters and made speeches. Approximately 100 people watched the protest, which ended peacefully.

Previous protests in Myanmar have not ended peacefully. In 2007, monks made a protest that was put down by the government, during which 31 people were killed.

Activity C

1 In groups, think about what kinds of things would be most helpful to end conflict around the world.

2 Produce a questionnaire to find out what other people think would end conflict. Then ask adults and other pupils to complete your questionnaire.

3 Study the results of your questionnaire and make a recommendation as to what Buddhists could do to try to prevent conflict.

Buddhist monks think non-violent protest is better than violent conflict, and they take part in peaceful marches and sitting protests in attempts to demonstrate their opinions and restore peace.

Activity D

1 Produce a poster or PowerPoint presentation to encourage people to support Buddhists who work to prevent war and conflict.

2 Include in your poster or presentation a description of what the work to end conflict could involve and some Buddhist reasons why it is good to work to prevent conflict from occurring.

The big assignment

Task

Produce a board game about ethics and ethical issues.

Objectives

- To investigate the ethics and Buddhist teachings about examples of ethical issues.
- To use evidence from Buddhist texts, Buddhist leaders and worshippers to inform your findings.

Outcome

To produce a board game that can be used by Key Stage 3 pupils to introduce ethical studies.

You should include information about:

- what ethics is
- what moral decisions are
- how moral decisions are made
- what human rights are
- examples of moral issues
- Buddhist teachings about different moral issues
- why Buddhists might make different decisions about moral issues.

Guidance

1 Work in groups of six or seven people. Each person should be given a specific job to do, and the rest of the group should support them in doing it.

2 Suggested jobs:

 a Asking Buddhists to help you with the big assignment.
 b Writing questions to ask the different Buddhists.
 c Research into: What kinds of issues should be included in the board game? What kind of board game should your group produce? How are you going to produce the board game?
 d Finding Buddhist teachings about the ethical issues through web-based research and library research.
 e Taking photographs or drawing illustrations to go onto the board game.
 f Planning the layout of the board game to ensure that sufficient space is given for the various parts and that the game will 'work'.
 g Putting the board game together and checking that the game works.

3 As a group, go through the outcomes of each job, and decide what needs to be done to finish it.

4 Remember to include instructions for the board game about how it should be played.

5 Your completed board game should contain: information, drawings, photographs, playing pieces and text.

6 Present your board game to a group of 9–10 year-olds, and ask them to play it and give your group some feedback.

Assessment

You will be assessed on:

✓ how well you use specialist vocabulary

✓ your ability to explain moral issues

✓ your ability to explain how important making moral decisions is for Buddhists

✓ how you allocated roles when making the game, and how well you worked with others

✓ your evaluation of the success of your team.

Glossary

activist a person who expresses their beliefs by getting actively involved

Bhavacakka (Bhavacakra) the Wheel of Life

bhikkhu (bhikshu) Buddhist monk

bhikkhuni (bhikshuni) Buddhist nun

Bodhi tree the wisdom tree; the Buddha sat beneath a Bodhi tree when he was enlightened

Bodhisatta (Bodhisattva) a wise person who has delayed enlightenment in order to teach others

Buddha an enlightened being; also used to refer to the first Buddha in recorded history, Siddattha Gotama (Siddhartha Gautama)

climate change a permanent change in the world's weather patterns

compassion sympathy and concern for the wellbeing of others

compassionate showing sympathy and concern for others

Dhamma (Dharma) universal truth and law

dukkha (duhkha) suffering

enlightened being a person who has found the way to overcome suffering and achieve perfect happiness

enlightenment understanding the truth about life

festivals times of religious celebration

Five Precepts guidelines for behaviour

Four Noble Truths the four central beliefs of Buddhism: suffering; the cause of suffering; the end of suffering; the way to end suffering

Four Sights scenes the Buddha saw as a young prince that led to his search for the Middle Way

global warming the term given to the increase in temperature of the Earth's atmosphere

intoxicated being under the influence of something so that you cannot think clearly

kamma (karma) the idea that a person's actions affect what will happen to them in the future

khandha (skandha) the five things that are the basis of what people understand as 'self'

lay Buddhists Buddhists who are not monks or nuns

magga (marga) (*see* the Middle Way)

Mahayana the largest Buddhist group today; also referred to as the 'Great Vehicle'; Mahayanan Buddhists are mostly found in North Asia, e.g. India and China

mala Buddhist prayer beads used to help concentrate the mind during puja

mandala a geometrical pattern created to represent life

mantra a word or phrase that is repeated in worship

meditate thinking deeply, usually to concentrate on a religious thought

merit the reward for good deeds

metta (maitri) loving-kindness

Middle Way a way of life where a person does not rely on luxuries to make them happy but does not go without basic needs either

mudda (mudra) a symbolic hand gesture

nirodha the end of suffering (release from suffering)

nibbana (nirvana) the state of having overcome desires and suffering

Noble Eightfold Path the way to end suffering outlined by the Buddha

oral tradition when information is passed on by word of mouth, often in stories or in song

Pali Canon Theravadin Buddhist scriptures

Parinibbana (Parinirvana) the death of someone who has already been enlightened

pollution contamination of the natural environment

poverty lack or shortage of money

puja worship or veneration, showing deep respect for an object or person

relic an item kept as an object to be revered

samsara the cycle of birth, life, death and rebirth

samudaya suffering which has a cause

Sangha (1) all those people who follow the teachings of the Buddha (the Dhamma); (2) Buddhist monks (bhikkhus) and nuns (bhikkhunis)

sentient the ability to feel and think things consciously

soul the spiritual part of a being

stupa dome-shaped structure used for veneration of the Buddha

Theravada a form of Buddhism that follows the teachings of the Pali Cannon; also referred to as the 'way of the elders'; Theravadin Buddhists are mostly found in South East Asia, e.g. Sri Lanka and Myanmar

Three Jewels the three parts of Buddhist belief that a Buddhist takes refuge in (Buddha, Dhamma, Sangha)

Three Poisons the root or cause of all suffering, greed, anger and ignorance

Tipitaka (Tripitaka) the three baskets, a collection of scriptures used by Buddhists

vihara a Buddhist temple or monastery

vinaya the rules for Buddhist monks and nuns

Wesak the full moon festival

worship ceremonies and prayers that show devotion

Index

Acknowledgements

For my children, Hannah, Laura, Ben and Rachel, husband, Richard, and Mum, Nancy, with love.

The Publishers would like to thank the following for permission to reproduce copyright material:

Photo credits
p.4 © imagebroker.net / SuperStock; **p.6** *l* © Photodisc/Getty Images, *r* © age fotostock / SuperStock; **p.7** *t* © kelvinchuah – Fotolia, *b* © Antonio Oquias – Fotolia; **p.8** © Jochen Tack / Alamy; **p.9** © Sipa Press / Rex Features; **p.12** © 1996 D. Normark/Photodisc/Getty Images; **p.13** *t* © stockerman – Fotolia, *b* © Studio9 / Alamy; **p.14** *t* © akg-images / Erich Lessing, *b* © 1996 T. O'Keefe/Photodisc/Getty Images; **p.17** © nuiiko – Fotolia; **p.18** *t* © sludgepulper / http://www.flickr.com/photos/sludgeulper/6064610160/sizes/o/in/photostream/ http:// creativecommons.org/licenses/by-sa/2.0/, *b* Courtesy of Birmingham Buddhist Vihara; **p.21** *t* © Yuli Seperi / Demotix / Corbis, *r* © Farjana KHAN GODHULY/AFP/Getty Images, *b* © Myimagefiles / Alamy, *l* © Sipa Press / Rex Features; **p.22** *t* © PORNCHAI KITTIWONGSAKUL/AFP/Getty Images, *r* © Lonely Planet Images / Alamy, *b* © Daniel Thory / Rex Features; **p.24–25** © Tyler Olson – Fotolia; **p.28–29** © Wolfgang Heidl – Fotolia; **p.34** *l* © Lebrecht Music and Arts Photo Library / Alamy, *r* © Robert Harding Picture Library Ltd / Alamy; **p.35** © imagebroker.net / SuperStock; **p.42** *far l* © Image Broker / Rex Features, *l* © Catherine de Torquat / SuperStock, *r* © Marka / SuperStock, *far r* © Akuppa John Wigham / http://www.flickr.com/photos/90664717@N00/147088970/sizes/o/in/ photostream/ http://creativecommons.org/licenses/by/2.0/; **p.44–45** © Imagestate Media (John Foxx); **p.53** © Sinopix / Rex Features; **p.55** © Bogdan Wankowicz – Fotolia; **p.56** © Chris Bright / Earthsangha; **p.58** *tl* © ColorBlind Images/Blend Images/Getty Images, *tr* © .shock – Fotolia, *bl* © Joe Gough – Fotolia, *br* © Ingram Publishing Limited; **p.59** *tl* © Radius / SuperStock, *bl* © Monkey Business – Fotolia, *r* © Monkey Business – Fotolia; **p.62** © Dondi Tawatao/Getty Images; **p.63** © Herve BRUHAT/RAPHO/Getty Images; **p.65** © epa/Corbis; **p.66–67** © Miramiska – Fotolia.

Every effort has been made to trace all copyright holders, but if any have been inadvertently overlooked the Publishers will be pleased to make the necessary arrangements at the first opportunity.